The Itchen Navigation

by

Edwin Course

ISBN 0 905280 06 7

Published by the Southampton University
Industrial Archaeology Group
January 1983

Printed by The Friary Press Limited, The Grove Trading Estate, Dorchester, Dorset.

ACKNOWLEDGEMENTS

I am indebted to the Record Offices of Hampshire, Southampton, Winchester and the House of Lords, for making available the records of the Navigation. I have also received valuable information from Mr. Mobbs, formerly of the Hampshire River Board. For helpful comments on the manuscript I am grateful to Lawrence Cameron, Christopher Corcoran, Charles Hadfield, Peter Oates, Laurie Pearce and John Silman. Pamela Moore assisted in assembling the material and also typed the manuscript.

Of the illustrations, all are by the author except the following to whom grateful acknowledgement is made – Cover, and Nos. 1-3 inclusive, Hampshire County Record Office, No. 4 City of Southampton, No. 7 Frank Cottrill, No. 43 Winchester City Library, No. 51 Ruthven Hall, Nos. 56 and 57 City of Winchester, Nos. 44, 45, 50, 53, 54 and 55 Winchester College, as is the frontispiece.

NOTE ON ILLUSTRATIONS 45, 50 AND THE FRONTISPIECE

These photographs are from College 'Notions' books of the late Victorian period. These are manuscript word books, compiled by boys, of College slang, ('Notions') and College names for the area – for example, St. Catherine Lock on the Navigation is referred to as 'First Pot'. Some 'Notions' books are beautifully illustrated with manuscript maps of the area and pen and ink sketches. Some have photographs which, from the text, are clearly contemporary with the manuscript. It is not known who was the photographer for any of these prints – they may have been taken by the boys themselves, or acquired from other sources, in which case they may be earlier than the books in which they appear.

(Information supplied by Dr. J. M. Gregory, who brought these photographs to the notice of the author.)

Frontispiece. Tunbridge in the 1870s, with the Navigation being used for recreational purposes – bathing and boating, while children look on from the bridge.

3

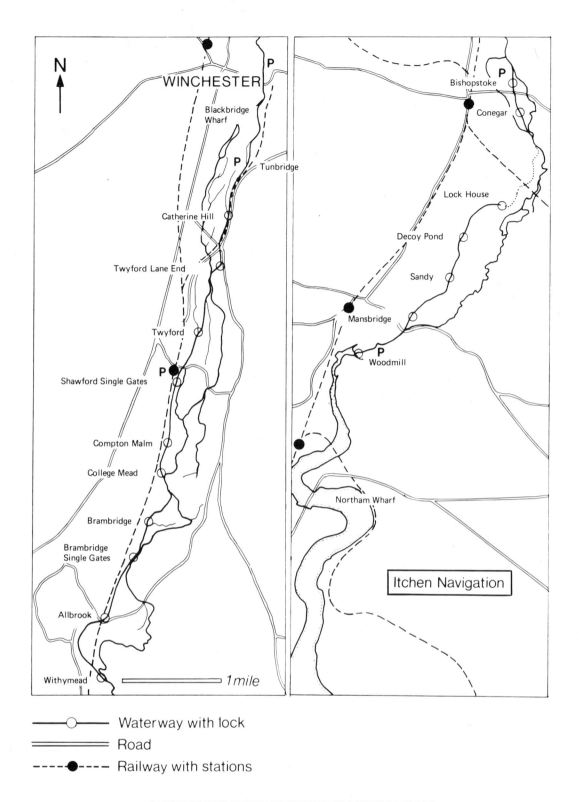

N

WINCHESTER

Blackbridge Wharf

P

Tunbridge

Catherine Hill

Twyford Lane End

Twyford

Shawford Single Gates

P

Compton Malm

College Mead

Brambridge

Brambridge Single Gates

Allbrook

Withymead

1 mile

Bishopstoke

P

Conegar

Lock House

Decoy Pond

Sandy

Mansbridge

Woodmill

P

Northam Wharf

Itchen Navigation

———○——— Waterway with lock

═══════ Road

-----●----- Railway with stations

ACCESS TO THE ITCHEN NAVIGATION

The Itchen Navigation may be walked either with the aid of public transport, or by a combination of private and public transport. Recommended access points are Woodmill, Bishopstoke, Shawford, and Blackbridge Wharf, Winchester. The distance from Woodmill to Bishopstoke is 3½ miles, on to Shawford 4¼ miles, and to Blackbridge 2⅝ miles, making a total of 10⅜ miles. If it is decided to walk the full length of the Navigation, this can be achieved comfortably in one day, and a break at the Victoria Inn, Allbrook, which is roughly equidistant from either end, is recommended. Alternatively, any one of the sections mentioned above makes an attractive walk. Cars may be left in the car parks at Woodmill or at Bishopstoke, and the return journey to collect them, made by train. Swaythling Station is about half a mile from Woodmill, and Eastleigh Station, a quarter of a mile from Bishopstoke Recreation Ground car park. Shawford Station is very close to the Navigation. Blackbridge Wharf is, perhaps, the least accessible of the contact points, being about half a mile from Winchester Bus Station, and nearly a mile from the railway station. Trains usually call at Swaythling, Eastleigh, Shawford and Winchester at hourly intervals.

INTRODUCTION

The development of land transport by road and rail has taken most of the traffic from the inland waterways of Britain. In the past they provided the easiest means of moving heavy and bulky goods such as coal and timber, but the combined competition of coastal steamers, railways and mechanised road transport has taken much of their traffic and left many miles of abandoned routes.

There were two main types of inland waterway – the navigations, which were improved rivers, and the canals, which were wholly artificial cuts, sometimes crossing water-sheds with the aid of locks and other engineering works. Many navigations were completed in the late 17th and early 18th centuries, and many canals in the latter half of the 18th and the first decades of the 19th century. Because of their special suitability for heavy freight, they were more important and more successful in the new industrial regions than in the south of England. Many of the navigations and canals of the south were in financial difficulties before the advent of the railways; few of them survived to carry commercial traffic for long after these opened. The Itchen Navigation fits into this pattern, being authorised by an Act of Parliament of 1665, and carrying its last barge, loaded with coal, up to Winchester in 1869. Although the Act of 1665 gives no indication, it seems that some use was made of the Itchen for transport purposes in earlier times. However, the relics which have survived over the 10⅜ miles from Woodmill, near Southampton, to Blackbridge Wharf at Winchester, almost certainly belong solely to the period 1666 to 1869, with which this account is principally concerned.

The Itchen Navigation was chronologically typical of the southern river navigations, but distinctive in other respects. For instance, although the Sussex Ouse, and the Arun had ports at their mouths, sea-going vessels could reach Lewes or Arundel without the need for transhipment to barges. The Itchen bridges, however, and other impediments, prevented masted vessels of any size going far upstream, and although the works of the Navigation ended at Woodmill, its powers extended downstream to Northam. Its most important traffic was coal, transhipped from the collier brigs from the north-east coast at Northam, and taken up to Winchester. The quantity of traffic was never very great and was always unbalanced.[1] The Napoleonic Wars imperilled coastal navigation and drove traffic inland, the route from London to Southampton including the Basingstoke Canal and a land haul to the Itchen Navigation at Winchester. Proposals to link Basingstoke and Winchester by water failed to materialise. Even at this period of maximum traffic, six barges appear to have been sufficient to move it. In fact, the value of the Navigation lay only partly in its transport function; it was also important for winter irrigation and summer drainage of the adjoining water meadows.[2] This involved the manipulation of the hatches or sluices in the banks of the waterway, a frequent source of controversy between the proprietors and the riparian landowners and tenants.

Until 1802, the proprietors enjoyed the monopoly of providing water transport on the Itchen, by virtue of owning the waterway and having the right to exclude all other boat owners. Another striking feature of the Navigation was the far greater interest shown in it by the Winchester people as compared to Southampton. Although Southampton was represented on the Commission charged with ensuring that the powers of the proprietors were properly used, its representatives achieved almost complete non-attendance.

It is perhaps fair to say that the works of the Itchen Navigation were formed over so long a time as to be the result of evolution rather than a definite period of construction. The authorising Act of 1665 specified that the river should be 'Made Navigable and Passable for Boats, Barges and other vessels'. This was to be achieved partly by improving existing parts of the river, partly by improving irrigation channels and partly by new cuts. The work was supposed to be completed by 1st November 1671, but it is clear that it continued into the following century, being virtually finished by 1710.[3] The new cuts reduced distance and avoided mills, and by virtue of their limited width, gave a greater depth for a given quantity of water. Sufficient water to float the boats was retained by means of locks, but the owners of water meadows in winter, and mill owners at all times, were competitors for the water which was needed for transport, for irrigation and for power. At some stage a towpath was provided so that horse traction could be used for the barges. When it was decided to provide water transport in the rather similar valley of the River Test in the 18th century, mainly because of the concentration of mills, an entirely separate cut was made rather than a navigation.[4] The locks on the Itchen were spread over the 10⅜ miles between Blackbridge Wharf at Winchester and Woodmill near Southampton, and although in 1795 powers were obtained to extend down to Northam, they were never used. There is evidence that the somewhat uncertain surveillance of the Commissioners was insufficient to keep the various proprietors up to scratch, and although essential work was done, and some of the locks were rebuilt, there were intermittent complaints about both the navigation and the service provided by the boats until commercial traffic ceased in 1869. The end of the Navigation is as ill defined as its beginning. It continued to deteriorate for the rest of the 19th century, and systematic maintenance was not revived until the Hampshire Catchment Board started work in 1942. However, its powers, like those of its successor, the present Southern Water Authority, remain restricted to drainage work.

THE HISTORY OF THE ITCHEN NAVIGATION

Although the archaeology of the Itchen Navigation reflects its history, and nothing has been identified between Winchester and Southampton that predates the improvements authorised by the Act of 1665, documentary evidence indicates that traffic was probably carried on the river in the reign of King John. It appears that Hampshire had a pioneer of canal construction – Godfrey de Lucy, a most remarkable and versatile man, who was Bishop of Winchester from 1189 to 1204. Bishop de Lucy was apparently responsible for rendering the River Itchen navigable, not just between Southampton and Winchester, but as far as the town of Alresford, where, 'by raising a vast mole or head, he formed a great Lake, now called Alresford Pond'.[5] In recognition of the Bishop's enterprise, King John conferred on him by Charter the right to levy tolls on all hides, leather and other goods entering the river by the canal he had made.[6] A number of further attempts to improve the Itchen occurred, including one during the reign of Edward I, when a jury decided that the watercourse should be made narrower and deeper in certain places.[7]

The idea of navigation was certainly current in 1617, when the City of Winchester agreed to pay the expenses of 'Mr. More of Farnham for his paines in surveying the water work for the river to be made navigable from Southampton to Winchester'. Although Mr. More's report, a lengthy document, was presented to the Commissioners of Sewers,[8] it appears that nothing practical was done until 1660, when the Mayor and Citizens of Winchester petitioned for financial help to undertake work on the Itchen, for the benefit of trade and employment.[9] The Act of 1665 listed a group of seven 'undertakers', who, in return for

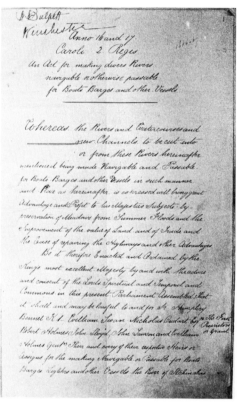

Plate 1. Page from the original Act of Parliament.

the grant of a transport monopoly, would carry out improvements on a number of rivers, those in Hampshire being the Itchen, the Test and the Hamble.[10] They were Sir Humphrey Bennet, William Swan, Nicholas Oudart, Robert Holmes, John Lloyd, John Lawson and William Holmes.[11] Advantages anticipated for the community included the 'preservation of Meadows from Summer Floods and the Improvement of the value of Land and of Trade and the Ease of repairing the Highways and other Advantages'.[12] To ensure that the monopoly was not abused, the Act stipulated that the cost of the carriage of goods must not exceed a moiety of the land carriage rates in force in 1663. Commissioners, appointed from the Justices of the County, were to confirm the rates to be charged, the proprietors having a right of appeal to the Assizes. All the things to be done were carefully specified, including the clearing and deepening of existing channels, and the removal of 'Impediments that may hinder Navigation either in Sailing or . . . Hawling of Boats with Horse or Men'. Locks, weirs and sluices could be constructed and the wharves and landing places could be equipped with cranes. New bridges were to be provided where new channels intersected roads or old bridges were obstructive. Of special interest was the right to make any new ways to bring goods to or from any of the rivers or wharves, and the placing of 'Footrails of Timber' which would have made these feeder roads embryo railroads. The towpath was to be on one side and only three feet wide, sufficient for men, but rather narrow for horses. There were various clauses for the protection of the community, including a requirement not to sever roads, not to demolish houses and to allow boats already trading on the river to continue to do so. The works were to be completed by 1st November 1671, failing which, the Commissioners could authorise the transfer of the monopoly to other proprietors. With regard to the details of the 1665 Act, it is worth noting that it was not confined to the Itchen, but applied to a number of rivers. There appears to be no record of work done on the other rivers mentioned in Hampshire – the Test and the Hamble – but the first proprietors failing, as mentioned above, the powers for the Itchen were transferred, on at least two occasions. There was a gap of about fifty years between the first definite proprosals to improve the river, and the virtual completion of the works in 1710.

It is clear that the 17th century monopoly became unacceptable in the 18th century, and in 1767, a hundred and two years after the first Act of Parliament, a second Act, instigated by three Winchester merchants, sought to remedy matters by appointing a new Commission, which was expected to be more effective. The Preamble states that the Proprietor 'doth not only demand and impose exorbitant Rates . . . but frequently refuses to carry and convey by Water, Coals and such other Goods . . . as interfere with his own Trade . . . whereby he has in a great Measure obtained and acquired the Monopoly of several of the Necessaries of Life to his own Use and Benefit, to the great Damage and Oppression of several poor and indigent Persons, and to the great Loss and Prejudice of the Inhabitants of the City of Winchester'.[13] This stress on Winchester reflects the balance of traffic, which was always upstream rather than downstream, with Southampton taking little interest in the Navigation. The Commission was to consist of the Mayor, Recorder and Aldermen of Winchester, the Justices of the County, the Dean of Winchester and the Warden of Winchester College, and was to be served by the Clerk of the Peace of the County. After an initial meeting in June 1767, they were to meet in Winchester Town Hall twice yearly in July and September.[14] Three kinds of charge could be levied on traffic – tolls for the use of the waterway, carriage rates for the use of the boats, and wharfage for the use of landing places. The first two were now to be fixed at Quarter Sessions, but wharfage charges were only payable if goods were left there for more than ten days. The teeth of the Act lay in the powers which the Commissioners held in reserve. For instance, in order to ensure maximum use of their boats, proprietors had usually only maintained the number that could be continuously employed, and this led to serious delays to vessels wishing to discharge into barges at Northam at peak periods. Now, if the monopolists failed to supply sufficient boats, the Commissioners could license others to provide them. Furthermore, they could authorise the construction of 'Locks, Wears, Pens for Water, Drains, Quays, Wharfs, Winches and other Engines, Landing Places, Weighing Beams, Cranes, Warehouses and other Works and Conveniencies'. However, no order they made was to interfere with the rights of the King, the Bishop of Winchester, the Town of Southampton, George Griffits of Epsom and his wife, Elizabeth, and Thomas Dummer of Cranbury at Northam Quay. Since 1711 the proprietors had rented the site of Blackbridge Wharf at Winchester from the Bishop for £3 per annum. This adjoined the road from Bar End to College Bridge, near the Bishop's Palace. The 1767 Act made the proprietors of the Navigation responsible for the repair of the road, in return for which the Bishop waived the rent of the Wharf, and instead paid £50 down and £7 per annum.

The Minute Book of the Commissioners, with its final entry in 1829, has survived and the complaints recorded cast light on the operation of the Navigation. The rates were fixed by the Commissioners, so these were not considered as subjects for complaint. Indeed, the scarcity of cases raises doubts as to whether the Commissioners were very effective in controlling the proprietors' monopoly. For instance, in 1786, complaints could not be considered because there was no quorum to hear them, so the Clerk could only send a warning note. The most common complaint concerned preferential treatment. For instance, in 1771, William Hooper, a coal merchant, stated that the proprietors, John Moody and William Meader, had brought up the cargo of the *Providence* from Northam before that of the *Witherington*, even though the *Providence* had arrived many days later. The fixed fine of ten shillings per ton of cargo delayed, as specified in the 1767 Act was levied. After a series of meetings at which no Commissioners were present, there was a sudden revival in 1793, when a number of complaints were heard against James D'Arcy, who had taken over the Navigation from Moody and Meader. A complaint that he had failed to mark his six boats with his name and address, together with their registered number, dimensions and tonnage as required by the 1767 Act was substantiated. Other complaints, including two from Moody and Meader, the former proprietors, were dismissed. In 1795, T. Deane of Winchester complained that D'Arcy had kept the brig *Swallow* loaded with eighty tons of culm, waiting so long at Northam, that instead of transhipment, the cargo had been unloaded on to Northam Quay. The Commissioners imposed the statutory fine of ten shillings a ton. During the Napoleonic War period, because of the danger to coastal shipping, the inland waterways prospered. However, the demands of the Royal Navy spread out from Portsmouth, and in 1793 the Mayor of Winchester issued certificates of exemption from the press gang to twenty-six 'freshwater sailors'.

By this time traffic was increasing, and the third Act, that of 1795, included powers to extend the works from Woodmill down to Northam, and for D'Arcy to raise more money and to replace himself by a committee.[15] This would have facilitated through traffic to the Salisbury and Southampton Canal, which was

Plate 2. Pages from the Minute Book of the Commissioners for the Itchen Navigation.

planned to reach the Itchen at Northam. There was to be a terminal basin, constructed on the site of the Roman Ditch at Bitterne Farm. The powers for providing aqueducts, sluices, locks, towpaths, etc., between Woodmill and Northam were never used, and therefore produced nothing for the industrial archaeologist. If they had been completed, there were clauses for compensation for damage to the mill and fishery at Woodmill, which were owned by the Bishop of Winchester. The financial measures included in the Act covered both tolls[16] and the raising of more capital. D'Arcy could either raise capital by means of mortgage loans or by selling shares; in the latter case the shareholders would have formed a managing committee. Like many travellers, the bargees appeared to have lacked respect for property, and a £5 fine was specified in the Act for any caught with guns or fishing nets. D'Arcy too was subject to certain strictures aimed at ensuring that the business of the Navigation was properly conducted. If he failed to provide sufficient barges for the traffic, for example, the Commissioners could, in the first instance, impose a £200 fine, and he could be subsequently removed for this, or any other offence deemed to constitute mismanagement.

By 1799 a report received by the Commissioners makes it clear that D'Arcy had not formed a managing committee and was failing to meet the obligations which might have justified his monopoly. Moody referred to five boats being in a bad condition; other complainants stated that only four boats were available, and that there were not enough horses to work them. Trade had suffered greatly from the detention of vessels at Northam waiting to tranship their cargoes into barges. The situation had been aggravated, as formerly, Winchester merchants had been allowed to leave goods on Northam Wharf free of charge, but now the Wharf had been sold to a company who levied charges, and the merchants insisted on coastal vessels waiting for the barges. The Commissioners ruled that D'Arcy must provide six boats each carrying twenty or thirty tons, with the necessary horses to draw them, or pay the statutory fine. At their meeting in June 1799, the Commissioners heard Edward Knapp complain that collier brigs were refusing to come to Northam on account of the delays arising from D'Arcy's failure to provide sufficient barges.

George Hollis was D'Arcy's agent. By 1800, in association with Harry Baker, a linen draper of Westminster, he had acquired all the 160 shares and assumed control, with Baker as a sleeping partner. Hollis gave up the idea of being the sole provider of barges, and expressed his intention of seeking Parliamentary power to abandon the monopoly and open the Navigation to all barge owners who paid the appropriate tolls.

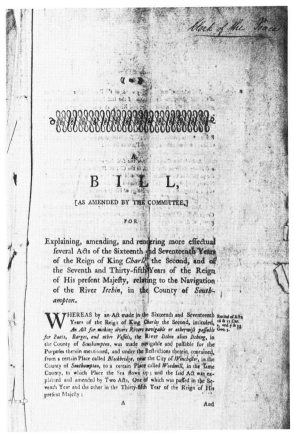

The fourth Act, that of 1802,[17] goes into considerable detail about carriage rates, about work required to bring the Navigation up to standard and about operating details such as rules for working the locks. Tolls on coal, culm, corn, iron, stone, timber and all other goods were to be at 1½d. per ton per mile. A full scale of carriage rates were given. For instance, a chaldron of coal from Northam was conveyed to Mansbridge or Gaters (West End) Mill (3 miles) for 1s. 3d.; to BishopStoke *(sic)* (6 miles) for 2s.; to Shawford (9 miles) for 2s. 9d.; and to Winchester (12 miles) for 3s. Wharfage for coals per chaldron and for other goods per ton at Blackbridge Wharf, Winchester, was 2d. with a surcharge if they were not removed within ten days. Many of the details are of interest such as the provision of mileposts to ensure that correct charges were levied, and the exemption from toll of chalk carried downstream by the barges 'when going for freight'.[18] As tolls were charged to the nearest half mile, 'stones or posts' were to be provided at intervals of half a mile, but as none of these have ever been found, they were either removed or else were never erected. A timetable was laid down for cleaning, deepening and necessary repairs – Decoy Pond Lock to Mansbridge by the end of 1802, Bishopstoke to Decoy Pond Lock by the end of 1803, and the rest by 1805. There was to be a fine of from £2 to £5 for depositing ballast in the Navigation; owners of sunken boats were required to refloat them.

As the passage of any boat through a lock inevitably used a lock full of water, boats of under twenty tons burthen could only use the Navigation with the permission of the owners, or by paying for twenty tons. Operating instructions were designed to conserve sufficient water for navigation, but not so much as to cause flooding. When a boat on its way up had passed a lock, the upper gates were to be shut, and the lock left empty with the paddles in the lower gates open, unless a boat coming downstream was in sight. As there were never more than about six boats in use, the possibility of disputes for precedence in passing through locks seems a little remote, but it was envisaged in the Act. The rule was that any vessel going upstream, which was within a hundred yards of a lock, had precedence. To avoid argument about distance, posts were to be set up a hundred yards below each lock. In cases where lock-keepers were provided, they had to observe these rules, and were not to decide – or be persuaded – about rights of precedence. All barges were to be registered by the Clerk to the Commissioners, and were to be of twenty to forty-five tons burthen. Presumably because of their interest in the transhipment operations at Northam, the Mayor, Recorder and Justices of Southampton were added to the Commissioners, but never seem to have attended. Under the new arrangements, three barges were registered in July 1802, and another two in May 1803. For instance Barge No. 1 was of thirty tons burthen and was owned jointly by W. H. Gater of West End, T. Black of Southampton, W. Earle of Winchester, J. Paul of Winchester, Edward Knapp, H. R. Hanley, Mary Ann Knapp and the Trustees of T. Knapp; Richard Walsh was her Master.

A meeting of the proprietors of mills and meadows dependent on the Navigation for irrigation, drainage or power was held at the George Hotel, Winchester in October 1808, and they arranged for a survey.[19] This was submitted to them by Richard Eyles in 1809.[20] Eyles pointed out that the 1802 Act had required the proprietors of the Navigation to put it in order, especially between Bishopstoke and Mansbridge, but this had not been done. He drew special attention to leaking banks above the locks, where the water was above the level of the adjoining land, and seeped through to lie stagnant in the meadows. Eyles did not attempt a monetary valuation of the damage caused by flooding, but he did assess loss of value arising from the Navigation depriving owners of mills and meadows of water for power or irrigation. The annual value of the mills was estimated at £1,000, and they would be useless without water, the water meadows valued at £4,450 would be worth £1,907 if deprived of irrigation water, and the Navigation revenue was put at about £1,000 per annum which covered operating expenses of £700 per annum. However, to put the Navigation in good order would cost 'upwards of £11,000', and if all the users of water were to be adequately served, this amount should be spent. This report evoked a vigorous defence from Hollis.[21] In 1809, the Commissioners recognised rising prices and allowed an increase in the charges on the Navigation.[22] These were enumerated in the fifth Act of Parliament, passed in 1811, which raised the toll on coals by ½d. per chaldron per mile. The proprietors were given another year to complete their scouring and repair works. The control of sluices and hatches had been in the hands of the Navigation, but a clause was included which gave the owners of meadows the right to open sluices to lower the water should a bank give way. In addition to the sluices, water was released over 'tumbling bays' when the level rose above normal. As there was no control over these, in 1811 Sir William Heathcote and Mr. Richard Goldfinch made an agreement with Hollis to permit them to draw the hatches when necessary to prevent flooding.[23] The sixth and final Act of Parliament was passed in 1820, and authorised a further increase in tolls of ½d. per chaldron per mile on coals, and ½d. per ton per mile on corn, salt, iron, timber and other commodities.[24] Somewhat oddly, in the same year that the tolls were increased, the Commissioners required the carriage rates to be reduced to those specified in the 1802 Act. The effect was presumably to increase the income of the Navigation and reduce that of the barge owners.

The 1802 Act had protected the rights of the proprietors of Northam Quay and the Corporation of Southampton by empowering the Commissioners to regulate the proportion of barges loading at Northam Quay as opposed to direct transhipment in the river, and in 1809 they required every fourth barge to go to the wharf, provided there was cargo waiting. They were also able to authorise the construction of a second wharf at Northam by the Winchester merchants. In 1824 the Commissioners renewed their ruling that a proportion of the boats should serve Northam Quay, subject to priority being given to perishable cargoes, such as corn and salt, over for instance, coal, culm or timber. In 1828 the Commissioners received complaints from Messrs. Knapp, Earle, Wells, Mant, Vaughan and Smith about the condition of the Seven Hatches which controlled the water flowing into the meadows between Blackbridge and Catherine Hill Lock. The last recorded meeting of the Commissioners took place on 1st May 1829.

How well the Navigation could have continued to compete with horse drawn road transport is unknown, because from 1839 it had to compete with steam traction on the new London and Southampton Railway. Because of well established links between the Navigation and various merchants, hope was sustained longer than was justified. For instance, in August 1850, a Mr. Forder wrote to the Manager as follows: 'There are two or three very important points which ought to be constantly attended to that the Navigation might be maintained in that condition which will enable it to contend with the Railway. The first is to keep the Locks and all the appendages in proper repair, secondly to lower the tolls equal to or rather below the charge of the enemy and thirdly to induce the mortagees to accept a lower rate of interest; by the operation of these propositions I cannot but think the canal may be made to stand against the competition . . .'[25] The railway intersected a loop of the Navigation at Allbrook, and the railway company's Act of 1834, confirmed by an agreement of 1837 between Hollis and the company, entitled him to £6 for every 24 hours in which the railway construction works obstructed the waterway.[26] The railway embankment came so close to Allbrook lock as to necessitate its reconstruction in brick at railway expense. In 1839, George Hollis transferred all his shares to his four children in equal quantities. His son, F. J. Hollis, who had been Manager and Clerk since 1832, was replaced in 1841 by W. W. Bulpett. There is evidence of considerable improvement under his control, for accounts were kept, and repair work put in hand. Writing in 1843, Turner P. Clarke, the Manager of the Andover Canal, refers to repairs to locks 'during the last year'.[27] He also commends the improvement to the banks and towpath but states that 'the benefit has been entirely lost by the non-regulation and consequent overflowing of the water'. In 1861, Mr. F. J. Hollis, who claimed to hold three-quarters of the shares, demanded that management be transferred from Bulpett to a Receiver. Probably in an attempt to ascertain if there was any future for the Navigation, Clarke was asked to make a report. This he presented in May 1863.[28] By this time only two barges were in use, and he estimated that their owners paid £250 per annum in tolls. £121 10s. 0d. he attributed to the letting of warehousing, stables and a Malthouse at Blackbridge Wharf. The Bishop of Winchester continued to pay his £7 per annum for the repair of the road, as required by the 1767 Act.[29] Mr. Wheeler paid £3 per annum for water, drawn off above Catherine Hill Lock, to operate his saw mill, and Winchester College paid £20 per annum for the privilege of bathing by the scholars. Another £9 was derived from rent, and small sums accrued from the payments of fishermen and pleasure boats, giving a total of a little over £410. The survey of the works which follows gives an invaluable picture of the Navigation in the last days of its commercial life, and enumerates and comments on the locks and bridges and the principal hatches. The attempt of Hollis to dislodge Bulpett failed, but Bulpett's victory was of limited value, as the declining commercial traffic finally petered out in 1869. The accounts for the closing years indicate how quiet the waterway had become. In 1865, apart from Bulpett there were two employees – H. Palmer, carpenter, paid £14 19s. 0d. for thirteen weeks, and J. Smith, waterman, paid £7 3s. 0d. for thirteen weeks. Other disbursements included £6 3s. 0d. to Mr. Newton for carriage of chalk, presumably for repairs to the banks and towpath, £2 2s. 0d. for weed cutting and £2 7s. 6d. for fire insurance.[30] Parish rates included £1 14s. 9d. for Blackbridge Wharf, 2s. 0d. for Compton and 2s. 6d. for Twyford. Tolls are enumerated, mostly for coal and salt from Northam to Winchester. Sand and building materials were conveyed from Chapel, near Southampton, to the West End Wharf, near Gaters Mill. The last barge, owned by Robert Newton, brought coal up to his yard at the Wharf in 1869, after which the Navigation slipped into gentle decay.

Mr. Bulpett remained as Manager and collected such revenue as was earned by non-transport functions. For instance, in 1872, the Southampton Gas Company paid £100 for laying gas pipes on the Navigation's property. In 1865, the Southampton Waterworks Undertaking was detected taking the Navigation's water. 'Southampton Waterworks Company having (as was now lately found out) clandestinely constructed a Culvert or aperture through the bank of the Itchen Navigation for the Water supply in connection with their works'. Mr. Bulpett's statement of petty expenses does not make quite clear where the offence was committed, as he charged £1 5s. 0d. to go to Portswood to see 'where the Southampton Waterworks Company had put their pipe into the canal', and later 10s. 6d. to meet Mr. Morgan and the Town Clerk at Mansbridge Lock to see 'the quantity of water taken out of the River'.[31] There was a reference to the sale of water to Southampton Waterworks in 1854, so presumably the water company had not considered it necessary to inform Bulpett that they were tapping the Navigation at an additional point. Apart from collecting what income there was, Mr. Bulpett had to stave off the aggrieved users of the bridges, most of which were beginning to fall down. In September 1879, the Winchester Highway Board gave him twenty-one days to repair Shawford Bridge. Bulpett replied that he had 'for years past been acting as an agent to what was once called the Itchen Navigation Estate which has for years been in a perfect state of insolvency . . . I shall be very happy to render you every assistance in getting it placed under the control of the County'.[32] The Highway Board carried out a temporary repair by shoring up the bridge in the middle of the span, Bulpett agreeing to bear the cost if ever navigation recommenced. In October 1880, Mr. A. R. Naghten, J.P., who had moved to Bishopstoke, threatened Bulpett, who by this time was a Deputy Lieutenant and a Justice, with legal proceedings because of the condition of Bishopstoke Bridge. Subsequently, it was decided that as the Navigation had no income and was without value, the Highway Board would have to repair the bridge. In view of this, it is rather interesting to find in 1881 Bulpett making a claim for damage done to the bridge at Brambridge by a steam traction engine. However, it seems clear that after about 1880 the Highway Board took over the responsibility for the bridges. By this time the question of ownership and responsibility for the Navigation was becoming complicated. W. W. Bulpett was Receiver, Manager and Mortgagee. As the mortgage loan was never paid off, when Bulpett died in 1899, at the age of ninety-two, his claim passed to his nephew, C. W. C. Bulpett. In theory, he remained in control until his departure to Kenya in 1925. In his dispute with Bulpett, F. J. Hollis had claimed to hold three-quarters of the shares – eighty himself and forty in trust for his sister. After losing his case to take over control of the Navigation, Hollis retained his shares and on his death, in 1881, bequeathed them to his nephew, R. M. J. Hollis of Greenwich. It is tempting to assume that the shares are still in existence, and in the possession of a descendant of Hollis, but efforts to establish this have not, so far been successful. In his role as Receiver, W. W. Bulpett made at least two attempts to sell the Navigation. In 1872, he was negotiating with J. R. Stebbing and in 1881 with H. F. Yeatman of Bath.[33]

The resurgence of interest in canals in the opening years of the 20th century did not miss the Itchen, and Mr. Downie of Alton produced a report dated July 1902.[34] It states that the Bulpetts as mortgagees, still held the right to collect tolls, and that it might be possible to purchase this from them. Mr. Patrick O'Carroll, a Southsea estate agent, claimed to have done this, and to have registered a company to take over the Navigation. He held a meeting at the Guildhall Winchester in September 1911, in the hope of selling shares.[35] This proved unsuccessful, and O'Carroll fades out of the picture. In the event, a mixture of people and undertakings took over. As mentioned above, the Highway Authorities rebuilt some of the bridges, and in 1942, the Catchment Board assumed responsibility for drainage work associated with the waterway. Various riparian landowners took over lengths of the bank, whilst Winchester College used the top pound for their rowing.

This development did not go unnoticed. For instance in 1911, Mr. Bowker of the Malms, Shawford, applied for a diversion of the towpath, described as a footpath. This was accepted by Hursley and Winchester Rural Districts, but rejected, following an appeal by the Rev. J. H. Du Boulay and others.[36]

However, a second application made in 1914, proved successful, although its validity has been questioned. Other diversions were made at Chickenhall, near Eastleigh and at Hockley, near Winchester.

Renewed interest in the towpath as an amenity arose in the 1960s. In December 1966, the Deputy County Clerk of Hampshire, accompanied by members of the Ramblers' Association and other interested parties, walked the full length of the Navigation (Plate 4). It was decided not to challenge the three diversions, but to invite the appropriate local authorities – at that time Southampton County Borough, Eastleigh Borough, Winchester Rural and Winchester City – to maintain the lengths of towpath in their districts. In 1976, the Itchen Navigation Society was formed, among its aims being the restoration and conservation of the Navigation. Before long, the Society found its aims threatened by proposals for the M3 Motorway, which would have obliterated much of the top pound. Peter Oates, their Chairman, gave

Plate 4. Perambulation of towpath of the Itchen on 4th December 1966. Deputy County Clerk, officials of the Ramblers Association and other interested parties about to set off from Mansbridge.

evidence at the Inquiry in 1977. Next came the threat of the M27, in this case crossing the line of the Navigation. The original proposals for the M3 between Bar End and Compton have now been dropped, and if restoration of the rest of the Navigation progresses, a diversion will be provided around the blockage by the M27. Unfortunately, the Itchen Navigation Society was, for a time, somewhat afflicted by extremists, but now has settled to its task of maintaining the towpath, and ultimately of restoring the Navigation in an effective manner. Meanwhile, the Southern Water Authority carries out its 'caretaker' duties and maintains a good flow of water along much of the Navigation. The Acts of 1665, 1767, 1795, 1802, 1811 and 1820 have not been repealed.

ARCHAEOLOGY OF THE ITCHEN NAVIGATION

It is possible to walk the whole length of the Navigation from Northam Bridge to Blackbridge Wharf, Winchester, in a day. The original towpath ran from Woodmill to Blackbridge and this can be followed with only three significant diversions. It was not extended to Northam, so although the Northam to Woodmill section did form part of the Navigation, it cannot be included in a towpath walk. This length remained tidal, with barges working up and down stream with whatever assistance they could get from wind and tide.[37] Until the completion of the railway bridge in 1866, the only bridge to be negotiated was the Northam Bridge of 1796 (Plate 5). The bridge's authorising Act specified a sufficient clearance for barges of the Navigation.[38] Nothing survives of the quay used by the barges or of the original Northam Bridge – the present, third bridge being opened in 1954. However, the railway bridge has changed little. It consists of three spans supported on solid abutments on each bank and by two pairs of iron cylindrical columns in the stream (Plate 6). The columns were filled with concrete up to approximate water level and then topped up with masonry set in Portland cement. Over the years, the decking has been renewed, but appearance and basic design remain unchanged.

Plate 5. *The Northam Bridge of 1796 seen from downstream about 1850. Note probable collier brigs at Northam Wharf, coach on bridge, and railway train on London and Southampton Railway.*

At Woodmill, although the site of the lock is readily apparent, subsequent developments have obscured it (Plate 7). This was the sea lock described in detail in J. Hill's report of February 1862.[39] It had been reconstructed in 1829 with the usual two pairs of gates to retain the water, plus a third pair, pointing downstream, to prevent salt water flowing into the Navigation when there were very high tides. A wooden bridge, fifteen feet wide and set at forty degrees to the line of the lock chamber, carried the road. Woodmill

Plate 6. *Railway bridge on Southampton and Netley line opened in 1866, viewed from downstream on 23rd January 1973.*

Plate 7. *Site of head of Woodmill Lock from upstream on 18th March 1982. The mill building is visible on the right.*

lock remained in use for barges going up the mainstream to the Mill at West End, even after traffic on the main line of the Navigation had ceased. Nothing is to be seen of this lock now, but it is possible that excavation would expose significant remains. On the section from Woodmill Lock to Mansbridge Lock, south of the bridge, the towpath has been upgraded to a metalled promenade, but north of the bridge it is ill-defined.

Mansbridge is one of the only two road bridges which have remained virtually unchanged since the end of barge traffic (Plate 8). Being a county bridge, it was not maintained by the Navigation, and is not mentioned in the various reports. It is a single arch stone bridge, constructed early in the 19th century. A temporary 'Bailey' bridge was provided just to the north during the Second World War, and in 1975, a new concrete bridge was opened on a similar site. The span of the old bridge at present water level is thirty feet and the clearance five feet ten inches, which may account for a need for barges going downstream to carry chalk or some other material as ballast. The bridge has been restored for use by pedestrians and is well maintained.

Above the bridge, the first length of new cut diverged on the west side, so, to avoid an additional crossing of the mainstream, the towpath was transferred from the east to the west side of the Navigation (Plate 9). To follow the Navigation it is necessary to cross the old bridge and to walk under the new Mansbridge. At this point, the towpath disappears, but there is no difficulty in crossing the recreation ground to reach the site of Mansbridge Lock. In Clarke's report of 1863, he records a wooden occupation bridge, which not only gave access to the meadows, but also served to transfer the towpath to the east side. With the exceptions of Woodmill and Allbrook, the chambers of the locks on the Itchen Navigation were not lined with brick or stone, so the only masonry or brickwork which may survive, is that which supported the gates at the head and at the tail of each lock. In many cases this has decayed, or been overgrown by vegetation to an extent which makes it impossible to fix the exact position of the gates. However, as a rough guide, the distance between the upper and lower gates on the Navigation is about 100 feet (32 metres) and the width between the walls supporting the gates is about 15 feet (4.6 metres). Needless to say, the scour of the water when the locks were filled or emptied tended to undermine the banks, and in some cases these were supported by a wooden or masonry toe although there is no sign of this at Mansbridge. The occupation bridge has been replaced by an earthen bank which crosses the lock chamber near the tail, with the remains of the walls supporting the upper gates above and those supporting the lower, below it. Of the four walls, those that supported the lower gates are almost completely obscured by vegetation, but the wall at the head of the lock on the opposite side to the towpath is visible (Plate 10).

Plate 8. Mansbridge seen from downstream in 1966.

Plate 9. Point of divergence of artificial cut from mainstream above the new Mansbridge on 11th May 1982.

Plate 10. Wall supporting one of the upper gates at the head of Mansbridge Lock, almost completely overgrown. View from towpath on 16th February 1982.

14

Crossing the lock by the earthen bank, the line of the towpath is joined on the eastern side, initially as a track, but after a short distance as a footpath of varying quality. Originally, because the water at the heads of the locks tended to be well above the level of the adjoining fields, it was embanked, and this was reflected in the level of the towpath, with a sharp rise adjoining the locks, and an elevation above the fields for some distance above them. However, parts of the bank are missing, so the present path does not coincide with the exact position of the old towpath at all points. The bed of the Navigation is clearly defined from Mansbridge as far as the crossing of the Eastleigh to Botley railway line, and although it has been drained, some parts of it are waterlogged. Because of this, where the next occupation bridge has been replaced by an earth causeway, a pipe is supplied for drainage purposes. The wooden bridge which was provided on this site, in common with some of the other features on the Navigation is referred to by more than one name – in this instance, Clarke calls it Sandy Bridge, but it was also known as Cow Pasture Bridge.

The next feature to be seen is Sandy Lock, which has survived to a greater degree than Mansbridge. The turf sided chamber has formed a dumping ground, in particular for barbed wire, which may have been part of the wartime defences of the adjacent airport. The walls at the head of the lock are just visible, but the brickwork of the tail is plain to see (Plate II). The pound between Sandy Lock and Decoy Pond Lock varies from being virtually dry at one end to very wet at the Decoy Pond End. The embankment on which the towpath was carried is about six feet above the adjoining fields just to the north of Sandy Lock. Decoy Pond Lock was named for the duck decoy in a nearby wood. It was described by Clarke in 1863 as 'out of repair', and although the head and tail are discernible, the walls have suffered badly from vegetation growth. In particular, the wall at the tail on the towpath side is fractured by a fully grown tree (Plate 12).

Plate 11. Damaged brickwork at the site of the lower gates of Sandy Lock on 16th February 1982. The lock chamber contains an unusual quantity of debris.

The wooden occupation bridges near Mansbridge and Sandy Locks have been replaced by earthen banks, but that above Decoy Pond Lock has not been so replaced, the only clue to its position being provided by a widening of the bank. The towpath embankment has not survived to its full height at all points, although it does approach an elevation of six feet north of Decoy Pond Lock. Along this pound, both the cut and the towpath are well-defined and may be taken as typical of this part of the Navigation (Plate 13). The site of New Barn Bridge, described by Clarke as Stoneham Farm Bridge, is marked by an earthen bank. The farm itself is disused, most of its fields being taken over by Eastleigh Airport.

Plate 12. Tree growing out of the wall on the towpath side at the tail of Decoy Pond Lock on 16th February 1982.

Plate 13. Bed of the Itchen Navigation near North Stoneham Farm looking towards Winchester on 28th June 1964.

Lock House Lock, sometimes called Chickenhall Lock, was distinguished by its attendant lock-keeper's house. The site of this house was in the patch of brambles on the towpath side. Fifteen years ago there were certainly traces of the garden, but now nothing is to be found of this isolated residence. The walls which supported the top gates of the lock are obscured by vegetation, but the wall at the tail on the opposite side of the towpath is clearly visible. Not only is it possible to see both the stone and brickwork, but also the niche indicating the position of the heel post of the gate (Plate 14). Beyond the lock site, the line of the Navigation is crossed by a track, leading to some premises of British Rail, but this is not on the site of an old occupation bridge. However, a little to the north there are indications of a bridge that once carried a railway siding over the Navigation. Beyond this, the path is subjected to considerable undulation owing to the erosion of the embankment.

In 1841, when the railway was opened from Eastleigh to Gosport, the Navigation was crossed by a bridge with two arches, one for the Navigation and towpath, and a second for the occupiers of the land (Plate 15). Like the county bridge at Mansbridge, this was not the property of the Navigation, and is therefore not mentioned in the various reports. By 1979, the bridge had reached a stage when rebuilding was necessary,

Plate 14. Wall opposite towpath at Lockhouse Lock, seen on 16th February 1982. Recess for one of the lower gates is visible on the righthand side of the photograph.

Plate 15. Railway bridge, near Chickenhall, with arches – one for the Navigation and one for the use of occupiers of the land. It was brought into use in 1841. This view was taken from the south side on 4th December 1966.

and British Rail decided that the most economical technique would be to replace the brick arches with an embankment. This was done, but with a concrete tube of sufficient width to accommodate the waterway if ever it should be re-opened (Plate 16).

The length from the railway bridge to Conegar Lock comes nearer than any other part of the Navigation to extinction. The towpath continued on the east side, while the present footpath is on the west side at varying distances from the site of the cut. Two lengths, one immediately north of the railway bridge, and another near the Eastleigh Sewage Works, have been filled in. Chickenhall Bridge, another wooden occupation bridge, was described by Clarke as in a bad condition, and no trace of it remains. However, although stretches have been obliterated, they are not long enough to leave the course of the Navigation in doubt (Plate 17). The present footpath skirts the perimeter of the Sewage Works and the right of way then continues along a metalled private road. A footpath leaves this on the east side, leading to a narrow

Plate 16. The replacement for the two arch bridges at Chickenhall, constructed in 1979, as seen on 4th March 1982.

Plate 17. Line of cut in foreground filled in and obliterated, but its position indicated by dried up bed beyond the fence. View on 4th March 1982, taken near Chickenhall Sewage Works, looking towards Southampton.

footbridge across Barton River. This was a millstream leaving the River Itchen north of Bishopstoke, and providing power for the now demolished Barton Mill. (The main river served Bishopstoke Mill.) The cut made a level crossing over the Barton River just west of the point where this rejoins the mainstream. What was once a 'diagonal cross roads' has now become a 'skewed tee junction', with the line of the cut occupied by a vegetable plot on the south side but carrying water to the north. It will be appreciated that north of this point the valley carries three waterways, the main stream of the Itchen, the Navigation cut, and the Barton River. At the level crossing between the cut and the Barton River, Clarke records both the Fish House Bay Hatches, and also a horsebridge carrying the towpath over the river. The hatches, or sluices, could be used to drain off excess water from the cut, into the Barton Stream. Now all the water coming down from the cut, flows into the Barton Stream. The line of the original towpath is rejoined on the east side of the Navigation, as far as the tail of Conegar Lock. From this point to Winchester, both cut and locks have survived to a greater degree than on the southern section.

Alternative names for Conegar Lock were Stoke Conygar and Coneygear. Clarke describes it as 'very delapidated' with the 'upper apron' (or cill) about to disintegrate, and a large shoal below the lower gates. Needless to say, the top cill has now distintegrated and in the absence of sluices, the 'rapids' have cut back for some distance above the lock chamber. Originally a wooden occupation bridge crossed below the lock, and this also carried the towpath from the east side, which it had followed from Mansbridge Lock, to the west side. The modern footbridge crosses the well preserved tail of the lock (Plate 18). Conegar was a turf-sided lock, but here erosion of the sides of the chamber was prevented by the provision of a brick toe, which still survives although it has suffered some decay (Plate 19). A survey of the lock site in March 1971, led to the

Plate 19. Chamber of Conegar Lock showing brick reinforcement at bottom of turf sides Constriction in middle distance at site of upper gates. Note the rapid flow of water reflecting the change of level once maintained by the lock gates. View from footbridge looking to Winchester on 4th December 1966.

Plate 18. Modern footbridge spanning the tail of Conegar Lock, seen from the south on 4th March 1982.

discovery of one of the heel posts of the top gates, below water level (Plate 20). In addition to the lock chamber, an examination was made of the hatches immediately above the lock which regulated the water supply for 'drowning' the adjacent water or floating meadows (Plate 21). These are perhaps the best

Plate 20. Heel post of one of the top gates at Conegar Lock, seen on 27th March 1971.

Plate 21. Hatches above Conegar being surveyed on 27th March 1971.

surviving examples of hatches on the Navigation, the setting for the paddle being constructed of well dressed stone, almost certainly Isle of Wight limestone (Plate 22).

There were five occupation bridges, but the first highway bridge above Mansbridge was at Bishopstoke, and this was the most southerly of the highway bridges owned by the Navigation. As already mentioned, when the Navigation ceased to maintain its bridges by the 1880s, the local Highway Board replaced them with fixed iron spans. It is unlikely that these would have permitted the passage of unladen barges – for instance the clearance under Stoke Bridge is between two and three feet, depending on the water level (Plate 23). From Stoke Bridge to the site of Bishopstoke (or Stoke) Lock, the towpath has been converted to a tarmaced footpath. Nothing remains of Bishopstoke Wharf. A Victorian drawing of the top gates of Stoke Lock, shows the water from above spilling over vents in the gates. The bars by which the paddles, one in each gate, were raised, are clearly shown, and also wooden piling in the chamber of the lock, which would both protect the sides, and also ensure that descending boats were not caught on the sides when the water level was being lowered (Plate 24). The photograph of March 1982 was taken at roughly the same distance from the head of the lock as the drawing, but from the western, or towpath side instead of from the path on the eastern side. The wooden piling has been replaced, immediately below the head, by a sloping brick wall, and extended with sheet steel piling. The walls which once supported the gates have been maintained to strengthen the present three sluices which regulate the flow of water. The modern footbridge which crosses the tail of the lock is not part of the Navigation (Plate 25).

Plate 22. Setting for sluice used for 'drowning' meadows above Conegar Lock, as seen on 27th March 1971.

Plate 23. The present Stoke Bridge, typical of the replacement bridges provided by the Highways Boards after the demise of the Navigation. View from the south on 4th March 1982.

Plate 24. A Victorian drawing of Bishopstoke (Stoke) Lock shows the upper gates as seen from the lock chamber on the side opposite to the towpath.

Plate 25. A sluice at Bishopstoke (Stoke) Lock occupies the position of the upper gates. As shown in this view, taken on 9th March 1982, the turf sides have been replaced by brick and sheet steel piling.

A short distance to the north, the mainstream of the Itchen is joined. While most of the Navigation consisted of new cuts or adapted leats, for about half a mile, between Stoke Lock and Withymead Lock, the mainstream was used, and this is reflected both in the cross section and the curvature of the waterway. Clarke uses the word 'bay' for waterway junctions, so that, after the reference to Fish House Bay (the crossing with Barton River), he describes Barton Bay which, as at Fish House, had a horsebridge to carry the towpath, and hatches to regulate the flow of water into Barton River. He summarises the condition of the bridge and hatches in 1863 as 'middling'. Both bridge and hatches have been replaced by modern installations. The towpath follows the west side of the mainstream, with water meadows on the west bank and woodland on the east, to the point just below Withymead Lock where the next section of cut begins (Plate 26).

There are remains of both the head and tail of Withymead Lock, with a weir at the head. The normal arrangement of Itchen Navigation locks was to keep the top gates closed and the bottom gates open, with any excess water flowing through vents in the top gates. However, at Withymead, a side stream was provided on the west side, to take off any excess water above the lock. The towpath changed from the west to the east side, and a modern footbridge is provided for the present path (Plate 27). The London and Southampton Railway opened between Winchester and Southampton in 1839, and a brick single arch bridge was constructed over the cut and towpath. Subsequent widening of the railway from two to four tracks was accompanied by an extension of the arch. The final widening came during the Second World War when railway capacity was being increased as a preliminary to the invasion of Europe. This broadening was carried on reinforced concrete beams rather than brick arches (Plate 28).

Beyond this railway bridge, the cut describes an arc and is crossed by the London and Southampton Railway for a second time. There was one wooden occupation bridge on this stretch, which may have been the last survivor of its type.[40] Ham Bridge, the present reinforced concrete single span, was built about 1950 (Plate 29). Another unusual feature of this section is the presence of houses with gardens running down to the

Plate 26. North of Bishopstoke (Stoke) Lock, barges used the mainstream of the Itchen, a section of which is seen here on 28th June 1964.

Plate 27. The head of Withymead Lock showing the weir and the modern footbridge, as seen on 8th March 1982.

Plate 28. Bridge carrying London and Southampton Railway of 1839 over the Navigation. Subsequent widenings of the railway lengthened the arch, and the final widening, completed by 1943, was carried on horizontal beams. These were nearest to the camera when this view was taken on 8th March 1982.

Plate 29. Ham Bridge, a reinforced concrete single span of 1950, which may have replaced the last of the Navigation's wooden bridges, seen from the upstream side on 8th March 1982.

Plate 30. The brick-lined chamber of Allbrook Lock with a weir at its head, photographed looking to Winchester on 9th March 1982.

Plate 31. The collars which held the upper gates at Allbrook in position have disappeared, but their anchorage survived on 9th March 1982.

water's edge, although surprisingly, few of them keep boats. As the railway bridge and Allbrook Lock are approached, although the embankment has been repaired with chalk in the traditional way, it is leaking in a number of places. Beyond the railway bridge is the site of another of the Navigation's highway bridges. This has been widened since its first reconstruction, and now encroaches upon the tail of the adjacent lock. Allbrook is unlike the other locks, having a bricklined chamber instead of turf sides. In fact, the original turf-sided lock was obliterated by the construction of the railway, and the present lock was opened at railway expense, probably in 1838. Its good condition is mainly attributable to repair work carried out by the river authority in 1944 (Plate 30). Not only is the position of the top gates indicated by the recesses in the side walls, but there are remains of the anchorages for the collars which secured their heel posts (Plate 31). There is a weir at the head of the lock where measurements are made of both the level and the quantity of the flow of water.

From a short distance north of Allbrook Lock, the cut is carried approximately five feet above the level of the surrounding land for about a quarter of a mile, forming an impressive, if not conspicuous earthwork. For a further quarter of a mile it runs alongside the mainstream of the Itchen without joining it. There were hatches both above and below Brambridge Single Gates to remove excess water from the cut to the river. One has been replaced by a modern sluice, with a small bridge to carry the path. Some of the brickwork of the Single Gates remains, and their position is clearly indicated by the constriction of the waterway. It has been suggested that the main purpose of the gates was to maintain a head of water for a mill at Brambridge which relied on the Navigation cut for its water power.[41] There would have been no great difference in level above and below the gates, and probably for this reason, there is no weir at this point (Plate 32).

The present bridge at Brambridge consists of a single span with an iron beam on brick abutments, provided by the Highway Authority and similar to Stoke Bridge. It was used to carry the towpath from the east to the west side. The lock above the bridge was usually called Brambridge Lock, although there are references to it as Diddams Lock. A drawing was made of it in 1880, from a viewpoint looking to the south from above the head of the lock. This was eleven years after the cessation of commercial traffic, and from this there appears to be very little water in the pound. It shows very clearly the design of the gates, including the

Plate 32. Site of Brambridge Single Gates, looking to Winchester from the towpath. Mainstream on the right; view taken on 9th March 1982.

Plate 33. Brambridge Lock in 1880, eleven years after the end of commercial traffic. The viewpoint is on the west side, from above the lock, looking towards Southampton.

vents for releasing excess water (Plate 33). Some brickwork remains at both the head and tail of the lock, and an unusual feature is the provision of an eel trap (Plate 34). North of the lock, Downs Bridge, constructed of concrete is a comparatively recent accommodation bridge. About a quarter of a mile beyond it, begins another short stretch – about a quarter of a mile – in which the Navigation used the mainstream. The arrangement is complicated by the presence of a relief stream running parallel to it, looking something like the parallel streams south of Brambridge. However, whereas at Brambridge the cut is on the west side, the towpath in the middle and the mainstream on the east, on the stretch south of the waterworks, the towpath is on the west side, the combined Navigation and mainstream in the middle and the relief stream on the east. Sluices in the east bank control the flow of water. Navigation and mainstream divide again by the intake of Otterbourne Waterworks.

Beyond this point is the second major diversion. The towpath continued along the west side to Shawford, but the present footpath crosses the tail of College Mead Lock on a modern bridge, and then uses a metalled track some distance from the cut. Although this diversion would seem to be no more significant than those at Eastleigh or Hockley, it has given rise to far greater controversy. The badly eroded chamber of College Mead Lock is visible from the bridge, and also the weir at the head of the lock. Malm Lock was another turf sided lock, the water level being maintained by a weir. The original towpath is rejoined north of Malm Bridge, but before it is reached, the footpath rejoins the cut on the opposite side to the towpath. Malm Bridge has a concrete span, on brick abutments, and replaces one of the numerous wooden occupation bridges. From the bridge, nearly to Shawford Single Gates, the footpath follows the general line of the towpath, although this is not precisely defined at all points. There are some particularly good views showing the width of the cut and the way it is set into the side of the valley (Plate 36).

South of the site of the Single Gates, some concrete pillars indicate the position of a footbridge, and there are relics of the abutments of a bridge. Unlike the Single Gates at Brambridge those at Shawford have been replaced by a weir. This together with the remaining brickwork and the constriction of the waterway gives a clear fix for their position (Plate 37). As with Brambridge, it has been suggested that their main purpose was to maintain a head of water for a mill, situated on a millstream diverging from the Navigation, above Shawford Bridge. In contrast to the mill at Brambridge, the building of Shawford Mill survives, although it is now empty. Shawford Bridge is a replacement, comparable to Stoke Bridge, and carries the towpath from the west to the east side.

Plate 34. This photograph, taken on 9th March 1982, shows the disused eel trap at the head of Brambridge Lock.

Plate 35. One of the few craft still floating on the Itchen Navigation. This weed cutter seen above Brambridge, looking slightly neglected in the rain, on 9th March 1982.

Plate 36. Navigation niched into the side of the valley, south of Shawford, as seen on 11th May 1982.

Plate 37. Site of Shawford Single Gates, showing weir and brickwork. View from north side on 11th May 1982.

From the junction with the millstream above Shawford Bridge, to a point near Twyford Lane End Lock, the Navigation used the river rather than an artificial cut. For about a quarter of a mile north of the bridge, the west bank is bordered by houses and gardens, on a much grander scale than those at Allbrook. The next feature of the Navigation to be reached is the lock known as Twyford Lock, Compton Place Lock or Compton Lock. The brickwork of the tail is plain to see, and is crossed by an iron footbridge (Plate 38). Of the three fairly short lengths of the main river used by the Navigation, only that between Shawford and Twyford includes a lock. It carries rather less water than the other two stretches as it is paralleled by the Twyford Drain. Nevertheless, it carries more water than the lengths of cut on which all the other locks are situated, and this, and the action of cattle drinking may account for the unusual amount of erosion which has worn away the sides of the lock chamber. So great is this, that it seems circular rather than rectangular. The position of the head is marked by a weir and some brickwork (Plate 39).

Plate 38. A winter view, showing the tail of Compton Lock, on 9th March 1982.

Plate 39. Weir and masonry at the head of Compton Lock. Erosion has produced this almost circular lock chamber, viewed on 9th March 1982.

Above the lock there are a number of relics of water meadows, including the remains of hatches. At Tumbling Bay Hatches (called Willow Mead Hatches by Clarke), the flow to the Twyford Drain is regulated. The present main sluices were installed in 1971, about twenty feet north of some 19th century sluices. When the River Board excavated the bank in order to construct the new sluices, they discovered the remains of the brickwork of an earlier sluice, probably of late 17th or early 18th century date.[42] Examination of the site shows some of the stonework of the 19th century sluice, still forming part of the towpath (Plate 40). About two hundred and twenty yards north of Tumbling Bay Hatches, the cut diverges from the river and the tail of Twyford Lane End Lock is reached. This is crossed by a wooden accommodation bridge. The east side of the lock is much overgrown, but the west side is relatively clear. There is a weir at the head, which retains the water level for some distance towards St. Catherine Lock (Plate 41).

Plate 40. Patch of stone in the towpath marks the site of the second sluice at Tumbling Bay. This was replaced in 1971 by the sluice visible in the background, photographed on 9th March 1982.

Plate 41. Chamber of Twyford Lane End Lock showing weir and site of upper gates. One bank badly overgrown, but on 9th March 1982, west side was clearly defined.

Plate 42. The bridge – or culvert which carries the Winchester by-pass over the Itchen, viewed on 11th May 1982.

Above Twyford Lane End Lock, is the third and certainly the most difficult of the three diversions, with the towpath virtually obliterated up to St. Catherine Lock. Initially the way lies along the A333 road to Hockley Traffic Lights, at which point, one is faced with the unenviable task of crossing the Winchester by-pass. Assuming that this hazardous exercise is performed successfully, it is possible to descend the bank on the far side to inspect the concrete tunnel which carries the Navigation under the cross roads (Plate 42). Nothing is left of the earlier road bridge which carried the Winchester to Botley road at this point, but some remains of a wooden accommodation bridge survive in the vegetation which borders the road. Just north of the tunnel carrying the by-pass road, is the railway bridge, on the line between Winchester and Shawford Junction, opened in 1891, and closed in 1966. For some distance, the cut, formed from a leat for 'drowning' the meadows, the remains of a local road and the railway, together with the dual carriageway Winchester by-pass, all run parallel.

St. Catherine (or Catherine Hill) Lock is the summit lock of the Navigation. A drawing by W. Westall shows the view from the tail of the lock in the early part of the 19th century (Plate 43). Later a saw mill was constructed on the west side of the lock, drawing water from above the gates and discharging into the lock chamber. Another view shows the head of the lock after the construction of the mill, with the water wheel just

Plate 43. Drawing of St. Catherine Lock showing balance beams of gates and wooden bridge across the tail.

visible at the end of the building, placed at right angles to the axis of the lock (Plate 44). Excess water is spilling through the vents in the top gates, in the same way as shown at Bishopstoke. Of particular interest is an early photograph, of the 1870s, showing the mill and the lock, with Half Way House visible in the middle distance (Plate 45). The water wheel and the gates also appear. Needless to say, the lower gates are open, which was not only normal practice on the Navigation, but also necessary if the saw mill was to operate. A comparison of this old photograph with a recent view of the tail of the lock indicates brickwork surviving, but the gates missing (Plate 46).

Plate 44. Drawing of St. Catherine Lock showing saw mill with water wheel.

Plate 45. A photograph, of the 1870s, showing St. Catherine Lock and the saw mill, with Half Way House visible in the middle distance.

As in the other locks, timberwork was provided to hold barges off the banks, and a bridge over the tail of the lock gave access to the saw mill. The chamber is still well defined with a weir and sluice roughly in the position of the upper gates (Plate 47). Just below the head of the lock, on the side opposite to the towpath, are the remains of the setting for the water wheel (Plate 48).

Plate 47. Chamber of St. Catherine Lock shows sluice and cill at the head, as seen on 24th February 1982.

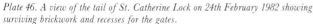

Plate 46. A view of the tail of St. Catherine Lock on 24th February 1982 showing surviving brickwork and recesses for the gates.

The pound above the summit lock has been used for many years by Winchester College for boating. The winding basin above St. Catherine Lock is just large enough to permit an eight to turn (Plate 49). No buildings remain on the west side of the Navigation, but Half Way House, a modest Victorian dwelling, appears in the background in the early photograph of St. Catherine Lock. A closer view shows its proximity to the Navigation (Plate 50). The towpath from St. Catherine Lock to a point just below Blackbridge Wharf is well defined, especially north of Tunbridge. This was a wooden occupation bridge which survived until

Plate 48. Site of water wheel of saw mill near the head of St. Catherine Lock, photographed on 24th February 1982.

Plate 49. On 11th May 1982, a rowing eight from Winchester College, turning in the winding basin above St. Catherine Lock.

Plate 50. Half Way House, situated about two hundred yards north of St. Catherine Lock, viewed in the 1870s.

about 1926 (See Frontispiece). An old photograph of the 1880s shows it, giving access to the water meadows. In the foreground there are signs of the construction of a railway line, probably the extension from the Didcot, Newbury and Southampton Railway's Goods Station at Bar End to Shawford Junction, which was opened in 1891 (Plate 51). The occupation road has now been upgraded to a public highway, and a new single arch concrete bridge was constructed about 1926 (Plate 52).

The length above Tunbridge is perhaps the best preserved part of the Navigation, with both towpath and waterway in good condition. Domum House is on the site of Domum Wharf. On the opposite bank was constructed the first College Boathouse, on the edge of an expanse of water meadows. Domum Wharf and the

Plate 51. Tunbridge in the 1880s with signs of railway construction in the foreground.

Plate 52. The replacement Tunbridge, photographed on 11th May 1982.

first College Boathouse have gone, virtually without trace, but the Old Barge Cottages survive. At the present time, the footpath leaves the towpath beyond Old Barge Cottages, leading into Domum Road. Between this point and Wharf Bridge in the days of commercial use, a storehouse was situated (Plate 53). Its site is now occupied by 'New Barge Cottage', and the present College Boathouse with a concrete slip on the line of the towpath (Plates 54 and 55). Wharf Bridge, dating from the middle of the 18th century, shares with

Plate 53. View of 1880s, showing Domum House, the first College boathouse, and the remains of a storehouse.

Plate 54. The corner of the old storehouse, Wharf Bridge and Blackbridge in the middle 1880s. The view also shows the end of the warehouse, and another storehouse at Blackbridge. The 'Alice in Wonderland' little girl admires the work of the artist.

Plate 55. Recent view from slightly upstream of Plate 54, showing Wharf Bridge, backed by the roof of the boat shelter, In the foreground is the slip of the present College Boathouse, with two boats about to leave for St. Catherine Lock.

Mansbridge the distinction of having been constructed when the Navigation was still in use by barges. It is a plain single arch structure, built of brick. The terminus of the Navigation lay between Wharf Bridge and Blackbridge. Adjoining Wharf Bridge a rather unsightly iron framed roof spans the waterway, providing protection for College boats which are not in the Boathouse. An early view of Blackbridge fails to show the type of wooden wharf which one would have expected to find. The same view shows Blackbridge with two arches (Plate 56). The present stone structure has one arch, and it may be that some degree of rebuilding has taken place (Plate 57). There are two striking survivals at Blackbridge, both of them restored in recent years. One of these is the former manager's house and the other a warehouse (Plate 58). Although it is probable that parts of the Itchen were used for transport beyond Blackbridge, this was the terminus of the Itchen Navigation.

Plate 56. An early view from Blackbridge Wharf, showing Blackbridge, the College Chapel and a barge with mixed cargo.

Plate 57. The site of Blackbridge Wharf on 18th March 1982, showing the bridge and the end of the warehouse.

Plate 58. The warehouse and the former manager's house at Blackbridge on 18th March 1982.

REFERENCES

1. The lack of balance between upstream and downstream traffic is reflected in the following amounts of toll collected during the closing years of the Navigation:

1866	Up	£160 13s. 8d.	Down	£15 19s. 6d.
1867	Up	£155 5s. 4d.	Down	£13 12s. 2d.
1868	Up	£122 17s. 10d.	Down	£7 9s. 4d.
1869	Up	£5 8s. 0d.	Down	Nil (HRO 13M48/55)

2. The 'drowning' of water meadows in the winter months brought on the hay crop; by late spring or early summer, when the water levels of chalk streams could still be high, drainage was important. The Act of 1665 refers to the 'great Advantage and Profit to His Majesty's subjects by preservation of Meadows from Summer Floods' (Preamble 16 and 17, Car II, c. xii) HRO 13M48/4.

3. The magistrates granted various extensions of time. In 1697 W. Bayley, gent., was given until 1700 for completion. Then the responsibility was taken over by a group of merchants, R. Soame, H. Gray and J. Stafford, who were to complete the work by 1707. In 1708 it was recorded that £6,110 has already been spent and a further extension of one year was granted on account of the delay caused by suits in Law and injunctions 'to stay the work' (HRO 13M48/32).

4. The Andover Canal 1796-1859.

5. Rev. J. Milner, 'Survey of the Antiquities of Winchester, Vol. 1', p. 229.

6. Charter Ri. John m.10. See 'Victoria County History of Hampshire', Volume V, p. 451.

7. Inq. a.q.d. file 4 No. 11 (4 Edw. I). See 'V.C.H.', *op.cit.*, Volume V., p. 451.

8. 'Hampshire Notes and Queries', Volume IX, p. 100.

9. Petition from Mayor of Winchester to Bishop Duppa, Bishop Duppa's Register, (Duppa LIBER QUARTUS), Entry 13, Folio 106.

10. 16 and 17, Car II, c. xii.

11. Sir Humphrey Bennet had presented a silver fruit bowl and a cup on receiving the freedom of the City of Winchester in 1660.

12. Presumably highways would benefit by the removal of heavy traffic, such as coal, to the waterway, while the delivery of stone for road repairs, might have been facilitated.

13. 7 Geo. III c. lxxxvii. The offending proprietor was Edward Pyott. The merchants instrumental in pressing for the breaking of the monopoly were James Cook, William Meader and John Moody; the last two mentioned later themselves being proprietors of the Navigation for a time.

14. Presumably the building now occupied by Lloyds Bank.

15. 35 Geo. III c. lxxxvi.

16. Rates from Northam to Blackbridge Wharf Winchester were as follows – Culm, Stone, Scotch Coal, Weighable Goods and Corn, except Oats, 3s 9d. per ton; Oats 3s. 6d. per ton; Coals 3s. 0d. per chaldron (an Imperial Chaldron weighed 1 ton 5½ cwt.)

17. 42 Geo. III c. iii.

18. The purpose of this is not clear. It could have been used as ballast by the collier brigs or it could have been necessary to enable the barges to get under the bridges.

19. The George stood at the corner of High Street and Jewry Street and was demolished after the Second World War.

20. A Survey of the Meadows and Mills from the City of Winchester to Woodmill taken by Richard Eyles, 6th February 1809 (HRO 40M78/23).

21. Answer to the Report of Benjamin Bevan and Richard Eyles by George Hollis, Proprietor of the Navigation, 1809 (HRO 13M48/2).

22. This appears to have anticipated the appropriate clauses in the 1811 Act 51 Geo. III c. ccii.

23. Sir W. Heathcote was concerned with the Navigation both as a drain to prevent flooding and as an irrigation channel. For instance, in 1850, Bulpett was proposing an annual payment by him of £200 for water taken from the Navigation for irrigation purposes.

24. I Geo. IV, c. lxxv.

25. HRO 13M48/54/20.

26. HRO 13M48/18.

27. Turner P. Clarke: General Observation 1843.

28. T. P. Clarke: Report of 1863 (HRO 13M48/31).

29. In fact the Bishop was already dissatisfied with the state of the road from Bar End. After an inspection in 1862, he decided to put the repair work 'in other hands' and despite his statutory obligations seems to have ceased making his annual payments shortly afterwards (HRO 13M48/54).

30. Mr. Robert Newton was a Coal, Salt and Corn Merchant and Barge Proprietor. The fire insurance seems to have been justified, for in March 1869, £20 was received from the Guardian Fire Office, presumably following a fire.

31. HRO 13M48/55.

32. HRO 13M48/23.

33. HRO 13M48/53.

34. HRO 13M48/32.

35. 'Hampshire Observer', 23rd September 1911.

36. 'Hampshire Observer', 21st October 1911.

37. Charles Penton, of St. Peter Cheesehill, Winchester South, captain of a barge for many years, gave evidence in 1863 concerning the construction of a bridge to carry the Southampton and Netley Railway over the Navigation. He stated that the barges never went up against the tide; they sometimes went down against it. 'I and the other captains of the barges sometimes used a Sail on the tidal portion of the river but it appears to me that the projected embankment of the Railway will interfere with our doing so for the future' (HRO 13M48/63).

38. An Act for building a bridge over the River Itchen at or near Northam, and for making roads therefrom. 36 Geo. III c. xciv (SRO SC1/9/10).

39. HRO 13M48/54.

40. Information from Mr. Mobbs of the Hampshire River Board.

41. Letter from Mr. I. D'Arcy of 2nd May 1981.

42. The present author has a part of one of the bricks.